Money Making Idea Book: Learn To Build Wealth, Retire Early, and Live Financially Free: A Practical, Simple & Easy Way to Make Money Using Stock Market

Copy Right
BLGS LLC
USA

All rights reserved. No part of this may be used or reproduced in any form or by any means, or stored in a database or retrieval system, or transmitted or distributed in any form by any means, electronic, mechanical photocopying, recording or otherwise, without the prior written permission of author or publisher. The information provided is for only instructional value. This book is sold as is, without warranty of any kind, either expresses or implied. This e-book is provided "as is" without warranty of any kind, either express or implied, including, but not limited to, the implied warranties of merchantability, fitness for a particular purpose, or non-infringement. In no event shall the authors or copyright holders, publisher, distributor be liable for any claim, damages or other liability, whether in an action of contract, tort or otherwise, arising from, out of or in connection with the book or the use or other dealings in the book.

This publication could include technical inaccuracies or typographical errors. Changes are periodically added to the information herein; these changes will be incorporated in new editions of the publication. While every precaution has been taken in the preparation of this book, the publisher and the author assume no responsibility for errors or omissions. Neither is any liability assumed for damages resulting from the use of the information or instructions contained herein. It is further stated that the publisher and author are not responsible for any damage or loss to your data or your equipment that results directly or indirectly from your use of this book. All products mentioned in this book are trademarks, registered trademarks or service marks of the companies referenced in this book. This book is not sponsored, endorsed or affiliated by any associated vender. If legal advice or other expert assistance is required, the services of a competent professional should be sought.

Trademarks: All trademarks are the property of their respective owners; BLGS LLC is not associated with any product or vendor mentioned in this book.

Why this book:

This book is for everyone who wants to quit their job and create a cash flow. This book provides easy to understand tips, tricks, ideas, solutions, formulas and strategies for financial freedom by investing in the stock market.

It covers following and more:

Learn How to invest in the stock market
Learn Investment Strategy to buy & Sell
Learn to limit your exposure to risk
Learn the Factors that affect share price
Learn to predict the optimum time to buy and sell
Learn Stock Market Indicators
Learn Market direction
Learn Stock evaluation screening
Learn Portfolio balancing…etc

Good Luck,
Peter

Index

Successful Investing Strategies: Step by step easy way to get started in the stock market

Successful Investing Strategies: FDIC Insurance

Successful Investing Strategies: Simple way to make money from stock market

Successful Investing Strategies: Easy Mathematics to make most Money in Stocks

Successful Investing Strategies: P/E ratio Techniques

Successful Investing Strategies: 52 Week High and Low

Successful Investing Strategies: Volume

Successful Investing Strategies: EPS

Successful Investing Strategies: Buy-Sell Stocks

Successful Investing Strategies: Easy way to make money by IPO

Successful Investing Strategies: Finding profitable stock

Successful Investing Strategies: Main stock markets

Successful Investing Strategies: Simplistic Techniques

Successful Investing Strategies: Types of stocks to invest

Successful Investing Strategies: How to know the value of a portfolio of stocks

Successful Investing Strategies: making money from market moves

Successful Investing Strategies: Making money in Bear Markets

Successful Investing Strategies: making money in Bull Market

Successful Investing Strategies: Knowing Risks

Successful Investing Strategies:

Successful Investing Strategies: borrowing money

Successful Investing Strategies: investing money

Successful Investing Strategies: Buy on Margin

Successful Investing Strategies: Best Strategy

Successful Investing Strategies: Dividends Math

Successful Investing Strategies: Amount of a dividend

Successful Investing Strategies: Value of the firm by discounting dividends

Successful Investing Strategies: Repurchases over dividends

Successful Investing Strategies: Information content effect

Successful Investing Strategies: Accounting identity

Successful Investing Strategies: Reverse split

Successful Investing Strategies: Over-the-counter (OTC) market

Successful Investing Strategies: Common Stock

Successful Investing Strategies: Stock analysis

Successful Investing Strategies: Refrain From Insider Trading

Successful Investing Strategies: Self-Directed Stock Trading

Use online broker that offers:

Successful Investing Strategies: Online Stock Brokers

Successful Investing Strategies: Pros & Cons of Stock Investing

Successful Investing Strategies: Economic Indicators

Successful Investing Strategies: Interest Rates

Simple Interest

Compound Interest

Successful Investing Strategies: Identify Stocks

Successful Investing Strategies: Tax

About the author: /editor/compiler:

Successful Investing Strategies: Step by step easy way to get started in the stock market

I. Opening an investing Account: Brokerage or trading account

II. Funding the account: Deposit Money

III. Buy Shares: Shares from your stock plan deposited into your account

IV. Pay Commission: Fee for trading orders to the market

V. Market Research: Best companies, stock trends

VI. Selling Shares: By placing a trade online or contacting your broker

VII. Settlement: For the sale and transfer of ownership

VIII. Money for the sale of the shares: Transferred to designated bank account

Successful Investing Strategies: FDIC Insurance

　　I. Brokerage products and services are not FDIC-insured
　　II. Brokerage products are not bank-guaranteed
　　III. Brokerage products may lose value
　　IV. Bank products and services are FDIC-insured up to $250,000

Successful Investing Strategies: Simple way to make money from stock market

A share of stock is ownership in a publicly traded company; Corporations raise money by selling stock in their company. Stocks are traded on stock markets.

A shareholder is entitled to share of the company's earnings.

Easy ways to make money from stock market:

　　I. Buy Low, Sell High: Profit = Revenue – Cost

II. Dividends: Money paid by a corporation to shareholders out of its profits

III. Buy Stocks That Pay, And Can Keep Paying

Successful Investing Strategies: Easy Mathematics to make most Money in Stocks

I. PE Ratio:
Price-Earnings Ratio (P/E): PE ratio helps in stock selection.
It's a ratio of a company's stock price to the company's earnings per share.
PE = Market price / EPS
Low PE means that the stock is cheap
A high PE means that the stock is expensive
A Lower PE always a better investment

II. Price/Earnings Growth (PEG) Ratio:
Price to Earnings Growth (PEG) = PE / Annual Growth Rate

PEG less than 1.0 means less prospects for future growth.

PEG is higher for a company with a higher growth rate

III. Dividend Payout Ratio:

The dividend payout ratio is the amount of dividends paid to stockholders relative to the amount of total net income of a company.

The dividends for stocks with dividend payout ratios between 60% and 100% are considered safer.

Payout Ratio = (Dividends - Preferred Stock Dividends)/Net Income

A high payout ratio is not sustainable.

IV. Price-to-Sales (P/S):

The price-to-sales ratio helps determine a stock's relative valuation.

P/S Ratio = Price per Share / Annual Net Sales per Share.

A business with higher sales but a lower profit margin indicates that it's not operating efficiently.

V. Price/Cash Flow (P/CF):

Price to cash flow (P/CF) is a valuation ratio used to assess whether a company is a good investment:

$$\text{Price to Cash Flow} = \frac{\text{Current Stock Price}}{\text{Cash Flow per Share}}$$

Lower readings are preferable

VI. Price-To-Book Value (P/BV):

Price/Book Value = Market Value of Equity/Book Value of Equity

This ratio will tell how much one is paying for every dollar of assets owned by the company,

VII. Debt-to-Equity Ratio:

$$\text{Debt-to-Equity Ratio} = \frac{\text{Total Liabilities}}{\text{Shareholders' Equity}}$$

Generally, the higher the ratio of debt to equity, the greater is the risk for the corporation's creditors and its prospective creditors.

VIII. Return on Equity:

ROE = Net Income/Shareholders' Equity

ROE measures a company's efficiency at generating profits from money invested in the company, and it is derived by dividing by net income by shareholder's equity.

Return on equity (ROE) is a measure of profitability that calculates how many dollars of profit a company generates with each dollar of shareholders' equity.

IX. Return on Assets:

A company with a higher ROA is usually preferable to one with a lower ROA

Return on Assets (Total Capital)

ROTC = EBIT / Average Total Capital, EBIT (Earnings before Interest and Taxes) is a measure of an entity's profitability that excludes interest and income tax expenses. Positive ROI indicates benefits is greater than cost

X. Profit

Profit = revenue - costs, so an alternative margin formula is:

Gross margin = 100 * profit / revenue (when expressed as a percentage).

Margin = 100 * (revenue - costs) / revenue.

Revenue: Revenue = 100 * profit / margin.

Successful Investing Strategies: P/E ratio Techniques

It's a financial ratio. High P/E ratio leads most investors to expect higher earnings.
P/E ratio =   Stock price ÷ Earnings per share

Examples:

Company	Ticker	PE Ratio
American Airlines Group Inc	AAL	3.86
Goldman Sachs	GSJ	2.4
General Motors Co.	GM	4.08
Ford Motor Co. (DE)	F	5.62
HP Inc	HPQ	6.04
Viacom Inc	VIAB	6.93
Dow Chemical Co.	DOW	7.75
Hewlett Packard Enterprise Co	HPE	8.53
Bed, Bath & Beyond, Inc	BBBY	8.54
Prudential Financial, Inc	PRU	8.59
Capital One Financial Corp	COF	10.04

Successful Investing Strategies: 52 Week High and Low

52 Week High and Low is a number that can help:
1. In determining the current value of a stock
2. In predicting a trend in a stock's performance
3. In determination of the predicted future prices of the stock

1 year = 365 days = (365 days) / (7 days/week) = 52 Weeks
52 week High: The highest price a stock was sold for in the past 52 weeks.
52 week Low: The lowest price a stock was sold for in the past 52 weeks.

Examples:

Security	52 Week High	52 Week Low
Teva Pharmaceutical Industries ADR	66.55	43.21
New York Times Cl A	14.27	11.45
Nokia ADR	7.63	4.88
Nordic American Tankers	16.68	8.94
Novo Nordisk ADR	59.00	39.03
Bristol-Myers Squibb	77.12	49.12
Brown-Forman Cl A	58.99	47.42
CVS Health	106.67	85.41
Adobe Systems	110.13	71.27

Successful Investing Strategies: Volume

The number of shares traded in a company's stock. Volume is the number of shares traded in a stock for a given period, typically for one day. When prices are falling and volume is increasing, prices will fall further
It's based on supply and demand.

Examples:

Sym	Name	High	Low	Volume
BAC	Bank of America Corp	16.23	15.94	108,865,594
TWTR	Twitter Inc	18.05	16.28	73,675,203
RAD	Rite Aid Corp	7.13	6.80	49,050,398
WFC	Wells Fargo & Company	45.52	44.32	45,418,598
TEVA	Teva Pharmaceutical	44.49	42.95	7,360,700
XOM	Exxon Mobil Corp	87.54	86.48	7,991,600
FB	Facebook Inc	128.95	127.58	13,345,200
PFE	Pfizer Inc	32.90	32.66	15,569,301

Successful Investing Strategies:
EPS

Earnings per Share (EPS) are financial ratio used by Wall Street in determining the earnings power of a company. Higher earnings per share mean better dividend and better overall Stock performance.

Examples:

Symbol	Name	EPS
ACC	Credit Acceptance Corp.	15.12
VDC	Vanguard Consumer Staples ETF	14.74
TM	Toyota Motor Corporation	13.66
GOOGL	Google Inc	25.81
IBM	International Business Machines	12.30
ICE	Intercontinental Exchange, Inc.	12.12
LMT	Lockheed Martin Corporation	12.01

Successful Investing Strategies: Buy-Sell Stocks

I. Stock Exchange

Contact a stockbroker, a regulated professional individual, usually associated with a brokerage firm, who buys and sells stocks and other securities for both retail and institutional clients, you tell your broker to buy/sell shares of a company. Your broker's order department sends the order to their floor clerk on the exchange. Buy and sells orders to a floor broker. Floor trader knows which floor traders make markets in particular stocks. The two agree on a price and complete the deal. A stop order to sell is filled if the market price falls to that price or lower. A stop order to buy is filled if the market rises to that price or higher

II. Electronic System

The New York Stock Exchange (NYSE) and the National Association of Securities Dealers Automated Quotations (NASDAQ) are stock trading platforms, they use Web sites to provide customers with access to
Trading online and information and answers to questions

Successful Investing Strategies: Easy way to make money by IPO

I. IPO stands for Initial Public Offering.
II. It's the first time sale of Common Stock in a public market.
III. Initial public offerings tend to start a lower price
IV. One can buy cheap IPO's and make profit
V. Investing in IPO's during bull markets can be a profitable

Successful Investing Strategies: Finding profitable stock

All high-yielding, dividend-paying stocks put more money in your pocket.

I. Yield: dividend earnings expressed as a percentage of an investment.
II. Formula for calculating yield: Dividend/ Current Stock Price
III. Find the highest yielding dividend stocks

IV. Low yield: High stock price low dividend

V. High yield: Low stock price high dividend

Successful Investing Strategies: Main stock markets

I. Primary market: Primary market is used by corporations to issue stocks directly to the public; the primary market consists of the issuer and the first buyers of the issue.

II. Secondary market: Secondary market is where investors purchase securities or assets from other investors, rather than from the issuing companies themselves, New York Stock Exchange (NYSE)

Successful Investing Strategies: Simplistic Techniques

I. Short-term techniques

Buy on margin: borrowing money from a broker to purchase stock

Sell short: Selling stock that you do not already own by borrowing then buying back at lower price

II. Long-term techniques

Buy and hold: long period of time

Dollar-cost averaging: buying a fixed dollar amount at a regular schedule

Direct investment: purchase of stocks from individual companies

Reinvesting dividend: use your dividends to buy more shares

Successful Investing Strategies: Types of stocks to invest

I. Income Stocks: These have history of paying high dividends

II. Growth stocks: reinvest profits into the business to grow

III. Emerging stocks: Young small corporations with higher overall

IV. Blue chip stocks: Company known for quality products and services

V. Defensive Stocks: remains stable during an economic decline

VI. Cyclical Stocks: Follows ups and downs of economy

Successful Investing Strategies: How to know the value of a portfolio of stocks

Yes, by using Stock Market Index.

Stock Market Index is a measure of the relative value of a group of stocks in numerical terms. It shows the performance of major groupings of stocks.

Indexes have been set up to track how a particular part of the stock market

I. Dow Jones industrial Average 30 largest publicly traded corporations

II. S&P: 500 largest companies in US

III. NASDAQ: Tech companies

IV. FTSE:100 highly capitalized UK companies in London stock exchange

V. Wilshire 5000: Measure of the overall economic health of the US market

Successful Investing Strategies: making money from market moves

I. With the help of Index Options, one can make a profit by anticipating market moves & Systematic risk i.e. day-to-day fluctuations in a stock's price.

II. Also one can use index options to hedge a well-diversified portfolio, spread out your money into multiple investments to reduce risk.

Successful Investing Strategies: Making money in Bear Markets

I. Bear Market is a Stock market that experiences a general decline in prices of stock.
II. Short Sale Tactic can be used when share price is expected to decline.
III. Short Sale is a sale in which the seller does not actually own the security that is sold.
IV. Seller will be Borrowing shares to sell, and then buy back at a lower price.
V. Purchases the shares back for less cost in the future and make profit.

Successful Investing Strategies: making money in Bull Market

I. When the economy is doing well, the GDP is growing and stock prices are rising its called bull market.

II. Buy and hold strategy. A long the stock, investor buys or owns shares of a stock with the intent of selling them at a higher price in the future.

Successful Investing Strategies: Knowing Risks

Market Risk: The following formula is involved in the calculation of risk premiums for stocks:

The capital asset pricing model (CAPM) is used to calculate the required rate of return for any risky asset.

CAPM can be used to decide what price one should pay for a particular stock.

Price of a riskier stock should be lower to compensate for increased risk.

The CAPM formula is:

$ra = rrf + Ba\ (rm-rrf)$

Where:

1. rrf = the rate of return for a risk-free security

2. rm = the broad market's expected rate of return

3. Ba = beta of the asset

Successful Investing Strategies: Measure of Systematic Risk, Beta

I. Stock with the higher Beta, have the higher expected return, as it leads to a higher premium thus higher return.

II. Systematic risk is associated with each individual stock because of company-specific events and risk.

III. Market risk is a good example of a systematic risk.

IV. A beta of one means the stock has low systematic risk.

V. Beta: helps to measure the level of risk in stocks.

VI. It's how sensitive our stock's returns are to changes in the market and how a stock's returns vary with market return.

VII. It gives a measure of how an assets return move with the systematic risk in the market.

   a) if B = 1, asset has the same systematic risk as the overall market
   b) if B < 1, asset has less systematic risk than the overall market

c) if B > 1, asset has more systematic risk than the overall market
   d) if B = 0, movement of asset is uncorrelated with the market
   e) if B < 0, movement of asset goes in the opposite direction of the market

Firm-Specific or Residual Risk component of return variance independent of market factor

Excess Return = $R(i) = \beta(i)R(M) + \alpha(i) + e(i)$

   a) $\beta(i)R(M)$ = component of return due to movements in overall market
      $\beta(i)$: security's responsiveness to market
   b) $\alpha(i)$ = stock's expected excess return if market factor is neutral
      i.e. if market-index excess return is zero
   c) $e(i)$ = component attributable to unexpected events relevant only to this security (firm-specific)

Successful Investing Strategies: borrowing money

When interest rates are low

Successful Investing Strategies: investing money

When interest rates are high

Successful Investing Strategies: Buy on Margin

I. Borrow money from broker to buy stock by a margin account
II. The margin in the account is the portion of the purchase price contributed by the investor.
III. The Margin Formula: Margin = Acct. Equity/Market Value of Securities.

Successful Investing Strategies: Best Strategy

I. Portfolio Diversification
II. Collection of investments

Successful Investing Strategies: Dividends Math

I. Dividends Distributable value: Shares X Dividend Rate X Par Value

II. Dividend per-share: Rate X par value
III. Total dividend: shares x dividend per share
IV. Cumulative Preferred Stock Dividend: shares x total dividend x yrs
V. Common Stock Dividend: shares x dividend per share
VI. Stock dividends: Dividend rate x shares

Successful Investing Strategies: Amount of a dividend

I. Dividend per share (Currency per share)
II. Dividend yield (Percentage of the market price)
III. Dividend payout (percentage of earnings per share)

Successful Investing Strategies: Value of the firm by discounting dividends

I. $V_0 = Div_0 + (Div_1)/(1+R_s)$
II. V_0 = Value of the firm
III. R_s = Discount rate

Successful Investing Strategies: Repurchases over dividends

Repurchasing provides a tax advantage over other individuals
Dividends are taxable to investors as ordinary income, Marginal tax rates 35

Successful Investing Strategies: Information content effect

I. Researchers know that share price of a firm usually rises when the firm announces a dividend increase and vice versa.

II. This effect signals increased future earnings and cash flows.

III. Managers often attempt to fool the market by increasing dividends; thereby increasing the markets estimates of the firms cash flows even though these may not be realistic.

Successful Investing Strategies: Accounting identity

I. Cash flow = Capital expenditures + dividends

II. Book Value of A Long-Lived Asset = Purchase Price - Accumulated Depreciation

III. Book Value per Share = Net Assets Available to Common Shareholders / Outstanding Common Shares

IV. Book Value per Share = Total Equity (-) Liquidation Value of Preferred Equity (/) Common Shares Outstanding

V. Over or Under Payment = Income Over or Understatement X PE Ratio

VI. Capital Turnover = Net Sales / Interest Bearing Debt + Shareholders Equity

Successful Investing Strategies: Reverse split

I. Older shares are exchanged for fewer newer shares
II. Reverse splits often occur when a company trading over-the-counter with a low-priced stock is trying to meet the listing requirements of exchanges.
III. Major stock exchanges have minimum dollar amounts for the price of the stocks they list. So, to stay listed, a Low-priced stock may reverse split in order to push its price to those minimums.

Successful Investing Strategies: Over-the-counter (OTC) market

I. OTC is a network of brokers who buy and sell the securities of corporations that are not listed on a securities exchange
II. Penny stocks are not listed on the NYSE or NASDAQ, they must be purchased over-the-counter, or OTC, leading many to call them OTC stocks.
III. OTC stocks are not listed on the major exchanges and do not operate within a central exchange

IV. Low-priced, small-cap stocks are known as penny stocks. Its good for Starting out on investment, high reward potential, There is very little regulation so its very risky

Successful Investing Strategies: Common Stock

Common stock is an ownership share in a corporation that allows its holders voting rights at shareholder meetings and the opportunity to receive dividends, the dollar amount of a common stock is listed in the balance sheet.

I. Income from dividends, cash or additional stock
II. Increase of stock value
III. Stock split growth
IV. Common Stock Valuation Formula

$$P0 = (D1 + P1) / (1 + r)$$

Where:
P0 = Current price of the stock
P1 = Price of the stock in one period
D1 = Dividend expected to be paid at the end of the period
R = required rate of return on this investment in the market today

Successful Investing Strategies: Stock analysis

I. Valuation by comparables: Size, Profit, Growth Profile, ROI, Credit Profile
II. Dividend discount models: Stock Value = D1/r-G
   D1 is the expected dividend payment one year from the current date
   r is the required rate of return
   G is the dividend growth rate expected to continue in perpetuity
III. Price/Earnings ratios:
   Stock Price / Earnings per Share
   Equity Value / Net Income
IV. Free cash flow valuation model
   Capital Cash Flows:
   Expected Return = Risk free Rate + [(Asset Beta) * (Risk Premium)]
   Equity Cash Flows:
   WACC = (Debt / Value) (1 - Tax Rate) * kD + (Equity / Value) * kE

kD is the cost of equity, and kE is the cost of debt

WACC is weighted average cost of capital

Successful Investing Strategies: Refrain From Insider Trading

Insider trading

I. Trading of corporations stocks or equity based on access to non-public information
II. To employ any device, scheme or artifice to defraud Make untrue statements of a material fact
III. Non-public information used to make a gain within the market
IV. Information comes from insiders: management, board, accountants, lawyers etc

Successful Investing Strategies: Self-Directed Stock Trading

Use online broker that offers:

I. Lower Costs
II. Lower Account Minimum
III. Best Features
- ❖ Stock Trading
- ❖ Options Trading
- ❖ Mutual Funds
- ❖ FOREX Trading
- ❖ Futures Trading
- ❖ Mobile Trading Access
- ❖ Easy To Use Interface Clear, Responsive, Efficient, Forgiving, balance, available cash
- ❖ Stock Charts Technical Indicators Rate of Change (ROC) and Momentum: speed at which a stock's price is changing. Relative Strength Index (RSI): Stocks movement in current direction. Stock Charts Technical Ranks (SCTRs): Based on a stock's technical strength. Basic chart: Yearly, Monthly, Weekly, Daily, Custom Time Period

Successful Investing Strategies: Online Stock Brokers

Online Stock Broker specializes in trading stocks.

I. Charles Schwab

Accounts from Schwab Brokerage   Minimum to Open

Brokerage Account (Individual and Joint) $1,000

Schwab One® brokerage or IRA account, plus:

Trading tools StreetSmart Edge® and Street-Smart dot com

Service fees: $01

Account minimum: $1,000

Commissions: $8.95 per online equity trade;

II. Fidelity

Fidelity Investments is the online trading brokerage, $7.95 for unlimited online, Easy-to-use advanced online trading technology

III. Merrill Edge

Merrill Edge is a full-service broker that offers equities and options trading

Building a balanced portfolio, $6.95 per unlimited online equity

IV. Scot trade

Largest and best known of the discount brokers, Regular stock trades cost $7

V. TD Ameritrade

Offers Powerful ways to place stock orders quickly conveniently, trade stocks online for $9.99 per trade.

Successful Investing Strategies: Pros & Cons of Stock Investing

Cons:

I. Volatility: The stock market goes up and down
II. Time-Consuming: stock investing is time-consuming because of continuous judgments
III. Difficicult: It's hard to find good financial advisor, having sound investment principles
IV. Emergency: It's not possible to quickly sell stocks to raise cash for emergency
V. Tax: more complicated tax rules

Pros

I. Abundant Choices: 1000s of publicly traded companies
II. Simple: most stocks can be bought and sold easily
III. Liquidity: Day traders buy and sell stocks on the same day by online tools
IV. Opportunity: for Substantial Returns

Successful Investing Strategies: Economic Indicators

I. GDP: Gross Domestic Product: Total value of all final goods and services produced in a country in a given year, formula for calculating GDP:

$C+I+G+(X-M)$
C=consumer spending
I=investment spending
G=government spending
X=export
M=import

II. Consumer Price Index CPI: Measure the overall cost of goods and services brought by a typical consumer.
III. CPI Formula :(Cost of basket at current prices/Cost of basket at base prices) X 100

IV. Unemployment Rate: the percentage of the labor force that is unemployed

V. Inflation: Sustained rise in price level. It means that the cost of living increases and the purchasing power of money decreases

VI. Deflation: Sustained decrease in price level. Purchasing power of money increases and households can buy more money w there income

Successful Investing Strategies:
Interest Rates

An interest rate is the amount of money a borrower promises to pay the lender.

Investing in accounts that earn compound interest will help grow your investment faster because Compound interest is calculated on the initial principal and also on the accumulated interest.

Here are the two most important formulas:

Simple Interest

$I = P*r*t$

I = interest earned in one year, usually
P = principal, the amount borrowed
r = the percent of the interest being charged (rate)
t = the time in years

Compound Interest

$A = P(1 + r/m)^{mt}$

r = rate
m = compounding periods
t = time in years
Future or maturity value

$A = P(1 + rt)$

A = the future value on simple interest
P = the present value

Successful Investing Strategies: Identify Stocks

A Ticker Symbol Is Unique Characters Used To Uniquely Identify Publicly Traded Shares

Colors

Green- Higher Than Yesterday,

Red- Lower.

Blue or White - Unchanged

Special codes at the end:

X – Mutual fund

Y – American depositary receipt (ADR)

Z – Miscellaneous situations

Successful Investing Strategies: Tax

I. Your deduction for investment interest expense is limited to your net investment income.

II. Any excess investment interest will be carried forward to the next tax year.

About the author:

Jay M Peter is an author & educator and he enjoys sharing his expertise on wide variety of subjects in easy language.

Reference, Copyright & Trademark Acknowledgement, Disclaimer of Warranty, No Liability Statements: THE INFORMATION, CONTENTS, GRAPHICS, DOCUMENTS AND OTHER ELEMENTS INCLUDED HEREIN (COLLECTIVELY THE "CONTENTS") ARE PROVIDED ON AN "AS IS" BASIS WITH ALL FAULTS AND WITHOUT ANY WARRANTY OF ANY KIND. Restrictions on use of content per Internet Privacy act. The content is copyright © BLGS. BLGS is independent training provider. All rights reserved. You cannot reproduce by any methods such as linking, framing, loading positing to blogs et al, transfer, distribute, rent, share or storage of part or all of the content in any form without the prior written consent of BLGS .its solely for your own non-commercial use. You may not change or delete any proprietary notices from materials received. We assume no responsibility for the way you use the content provided. All these notes files on this site are here for backups for personal use only. If you are sharing any information from here with any third-party you are violating this agreement and Internet Privacy act. General Jurisdictional Issues: Terms of Use will be governed by the laws of the Bucks County in the state of Pennsylvania in USA without respect to its conflict of laws provision. DMCA: All materials here are created with the good faith. All the references if any to copyrighted or trademarked materials are only for references and discussions. These notes do not replace any related vendors documentations. Readers are encouraged to buy and refer to the related vendors documentations and books. These notes are intended for personal use only. The use of any acronym or term on or within any BLGS product, content, website or other documentation should not be considered as impinging on the validity, ownership, or as a challenge to any trademark, logo or service mark. All other trademarks are the property of their respective owners, and the aforementioned entities neither endorse nor sponsor BLGS or its products. These notes or any material produced by this company is not sponsored by, endorsed by or affiliated with SUN,HP, IBM, and Microsoft, Cisco, Oracle, Novell, SAP,RED HAT,VERITAS,LEGATO,EMC,NETAPPS or any other company. All trademarks are trademarks of their respective owners. All these interview notes Content are not sponsored by, endorsed by or affiliated with any other company. Any Copyright, Confidential Information, Intellectual Property, NDA, or Trademark or Service mark infringements discovered on or within notes and the products and services will be immediately removed upon notification and verification of such activities. Please send your feedback to: bottomline@interview-guru.info Disclaimer: The information in this book is for educational purposes only and is not intended to be a recommendation to purchase or sell any of the stocks, mutual funds, or other securities that may be referenced.

www.ingramcontent.com/pod-product-compliance
Lightning Source LLC
Chambersburg PA
CBHW070419190526
45169CB00003B/1330